Copyright © 2023 by Amanda Clark - All rights reserved.

No portion of this book may be reproduced in any form without written permission from the publisher or author, except as permitted by U.S. copyright law.

Design and Publishing Assistance by Digimasterz.net

You can contact him at Digimasters94@gmail.com

This Book Belongs to

The first automobile was invented in 1885 by German engineer Karl Benz.

The first car produced on an assembly line was the Ford Model T, which was introduced in 1908.

Vintage cars are typically defined as those manufactured between 1919 and 1930.

Classic cars are typically defined as those manufactured between 1925 and 1948.

The first pickup truck was the Ford Model T Runabout with Pickup Body, introduced in 1925.

Vintage trucks are typically defined as those manufactured between 1910 and 1960.

Classic car auctions are a popular way to buy and sell vintage cars and trucks, with some vehicles selling for millions of dollars.

The first successful American car company was the Oldsmobile Company, founded in 1897.

The first car to achieve a top speed of over 100 miles per hour was the Napier Lion in 1909.

The first car to reach a speed of over 200 miles per hour was the Bluebird CN7 in 1964.

The Bugatti Type 57SC Atlantic is one of the most valuable vintage cars in the world, with only four examples known to exist.

The Ford Model A was produced between 1927 and 1931, and over 4 million were sold.

The Volkswagen Beetle was first introduced in 1938 and became one of the most iconic cars of the 20th century.

The Rolls-Royce Phantom III was one of the most luxurious cars of its time, featuring a 7.3-liter V12 engine and a top speed of 90 miles per hour.

Vintage cars and trucks are often restored and maintained by enthusiasts who appreciate their unique style, craftsmanship, and history.

The Mercedes-Benz 300SL Gullwing is considered one of the most beautiful cars ever made, with its distinctive doors and elegant lines.

The Cadillac Eldorado was a popular luxury car in the 1950s and 1960s, featuring tailfins and chrome accents.

The Ford Mustang, introduced in 1964, is one of the most recognizable American cars of all time, with its sleek design and powerful V8 engine.

Vintage trucks were used for a wide range of purposes, from delivering goods to hauling crops and livestock.

The Chevrolet Apache was a popular pickup truck in the 1950s and 1960s, known for its durability and ruggedness.

The Dodge Power Wagon was a military truck produced during World War II that later became popular with farmers and ranchers.

The International Harvester Scout was a compact SUV produced between 1960 and 1980, known for its off-road capabilities.

Vintage cars and trucks often require specialized parts and maintenance, and finding reliable mechanics and suppliers can be a challenge.

The Jeep was first produced for the military in 1941 and later became a popular civilian vehicle, known for its versatility and durability.

Vintage car clubs and events are popular among enthusiasts, providing opportunities to showcase their vehicles and connect with others who share their passion.

The Ford Model T was the first car to be produced on a moving assembly line, making it affordable for the average American.

The Porsche 356 was the first car produced by Porsche, and its success paved the way for the company's future sports car designs.

The Jaguar E-Type is considered one of the most beautiful sports cars ever made, with its sleek lines and powerful engine.

The Ford Model B was introduced in 1932 and was the first car to feature a V8 engine.

The Chevrolet Bel Air was a popular car in the 1950s, known for its stylish design and innovative features such as power windows and seats.

The Dodge Charger was introduced in 1966 and became an iconic muscle car of the era, known for its powerful engines and sleek design.

The Jeep Wagoneer was introduced in 1963 and was one of the first luxury SUVs, known for its comfortable interior and off-road capabilities.

The Ford Bronco was introduced in 1966 and became a popular off-road vehicle, known for its ruggedness and durability.

The Chevrolet C/K pickup truck was produced between 1960 and 1998 and became one of the most popular trucks in American history, known for its reliability and versatility.

www.ingramcontent.com/pod-product-compliance
Lightning Source LLC
Chambersburg PA
CBHW081125080526
44587CB00021B/3752